Tim did it

Written by Catherine Baker

Illustrated by Nyrryl Cadiz

Collins

Sid taps it.

Pam pins it.

3

Sid pats it.

Pam nips it.

Dip it Sid.

Pin it Pam.

Pad it Sid.

Tip it Pam.

Tim pads in.

Tim pats it.

pat

It tips. Tim sits.

Tim did it.

14

After reading

Letters and Sounds: Phase 2

Word count: 38

Focus phonemes: /s/ /a/ /t/ /p/ /i/ /n/ /m/ /d/

Curriculum links: Understanding the World: People and Communities

Early learning goals: Reading: use phonic knowledge to decode regular words and read them aloud accurately; demonstrate understanding when talking with others about what they have read

Developing fluency

- Encourage your child to sound talk and then blend the words, e.g. p/a/t **pat**. It may help to point to each sound as your child reads.
- Then ask your child to reread each page to support fluency and understanding.
- You could reread the whole book to your child to model fluency.

Phonic practice

- Ask your child to sound talk and blend each of the following words: S/i/d, t/a/p/s, p/i/n/s.
- Can your child point to the words in the story that have a /d/ sound in them? (*dip, Sid, pad, pads, did*)
- Look at the "I spy sounds" pages (14–15). Discuss the picture with your child. Can they find items/ examples of words beginning with the /t/ sound? (*teapot, teacup, toast, tray, tent, table, trifle, tablecloth, Tim*)

Extending vocabulary

- Ask your child:
  - Can you think of different words to describe the dragon? (e.g. *friendly, fire-breathing, naughty, mischievous, playful, fun, nice, funny, clumsy*)
  - The dragon is big. What other words mean "big"? (e.g. *large, huge, giant, tall*)